MR. DRESSUP'S
50 More
Things to Make & Do

MR. DRESSUP'S
50 More
Things to Make & Do

YEAR-ROUND ACTIVITIES FOR YOUNG CHILDREN

ERNIE COOMBS & SHELLEY TANAKA

Once again, with special thanks to Hildy Stollery of the Institute of Child Study, Faculty of Education, University of Toronto.

Copyright © 1991, 1984 by Ernie Coombs and Shelley Tanaka

Revised edition published in 1991 by
Stoddart Publishing Co. Limited
34 Lesmill Road
Toronto, Canada
M3B 2T6

First published in 1984 by CBC Enterprises/Les Entreprises Radio-Canada

CBC logo used by permission

Canadian Cataloguing in Publication Data

Coombs, Ernie
Mr. Dressup's 50 more things to make and do

Rev. ed.
First published under title: 50 more things to make and do.
ISBN 0-7737-5460-1

1. Creative activities and seat work – Juvenile literature. 2. Amusements – Juvenile literature.
I. Tanaka, Shelley. II. Title. III. Title:
50 more things to make and do.

GV1203.C67 1991   j790.1'922   C91-094800-3

Illustrations: pages 13 (bottom), 19, 26, 28, 29, 31, 32, 36, 38, 39, 40, 41, 45, 46, 47, 50, 51, 52, 58, 60, 61 by Heather Brown; pages 13 (top), 15, 18, 20, 21, 23, 30, 33, 35, 37, 49, 53, 56, 57 by Peter Grau.

Cover Design: Brant Cowie/ArtPlus Limited
Cover Photograph: Peter Paterson

Printed and bound in Canada

Printed on paper
containing over 50%
recycled paper including
5% post-consumer fibre.

Contents

Introduction

It's hard to believe that it's been seven years (and more than 600 television programs) since this book was first published. During those years I have acquired three grand-children, who share my love of "making stuff," and my co-author Shelley Tanaka now has another daughter, Jessica, whose sister, Claire, was our tester and critic when we were producing the first *50 More Things to Make and Do* book.

As we worked on craft activities with the children in recent years, we developed, independently of each other, many new ideas. Looking through the book, we could see that some of our original material could be replaced with what we considered to be better projects. Obviously it was time for a revised edition of *50 More Things to Make and Do*.

As in the original version, many of these activities can be shared by younger and older children, working together to make things and taking part in games, activities and situations. We hope that the activities in this book will stimulate children's creative abilities so that they will adapt these and make up their own variations. It's the sense of discovery that is important in these activities, rather than the final result. Let your children do as much as they can on their own and encourage them to experiment and work through the creative processes themselves.

Because holidays and seasons are so important to children, and in Canada our seasons are so distinctive, we have arranged this book in a seasonal format. We hope that this will give parents and teachers ideas for various activities that tie in with certain times of the year, although no particular project need or should be restricted to one day or month in the calendar.

Revising this book has been a great pleasure for both Shelley and me. Once more my dining-room table disappeared for days under a mass of scraps and found materials. In Shelley's rural Ontario home her daughters were delighted to be participants in the creative process of "book making." We hope that you, too, will take pleasure in the contents of this book as the year moves from season to season.

Have fun!

Mr. Dressup

Mr. Dressup

Things to Save

beads
spools
buttons
discarded costume jewellery
socks
nylons

travel brochures
magazines and catalogues
greeting cards
postcards
newspapers
paper bags
gift wrap
crepe paper
aluminum foil
waxed paper
corrugated paper
cardboard mailing tubes
envelopes
paper placemats
paper towel and toilet paper rolls
shirt cardboards
egg cartons
aluminum foil containers and pie plates
cardboard and Styrofoam vegetable trays
    and containers
juice cans and lids
baby food jars and lids
food labels
rubber jar rings
bread bag fasteners (square)
boxes (cereal, shoe, candy, etc.)
fine bamboo from discarded bamboo
    blinds, etc.
wooden dowelling
tennis ball cans and lids
paper plates and cups
styrofoam pieces, chunks, slabs, etc.
sponge pieces
cotton batting
ends of crayons
pencil stubs
elastic bands

pipe cleaners
twist ties
bottle caps
discarded pots and pans, metal baking
    utensils
fluted muffin and candy cups
hardware scraps (nuts and bolts, washers,
    drawer handles, door knobs, the insides
    of broken toys with springs, parts from
    broken televisions, radios, clocks,
    watches, old bicycle parts, hubcaps)
toothpicks
popsicle sticks
straws
tongue depressors
corks
magnets

ribbon
string
yarn
thread
cloth scraps
raffia
twine
shoe laces
clothespins
key rings

dried beans (lima, chick pea, romano, etc.)
macaroni
egg shells
seeds and pits
dried tea leaves
dried coffee grounds
dried kernels and berries

pine cones
dried leaves
sea shells
feathers
beach glass
stones and pebbles

Things to Make and Do in the Autumn

Metal Monster

Start the fall season with a family project that's both creative and practical. While the weather is still fine, make this monster over a couple of weekends and use it to help clean up metal odds and ends, outdoors and in.

Materials:
sturdy carton boxes (liquor store boxes work well—tape them shut and leave in the dividers for added strength)
discarded odds and ends (old bike wheels, hubcaps, bike chains, foil pie plates, discarded pots and pans, metal baking utensils, metal caps from assorted containers, metal door knobs and drawer handles, buttons, etc.)
newspaper, torn into wide strips or sheets
paste—lots of it
wide masking tape
wide paint brush
tempera paint or spray paint

Instructions: Using four to ten sturdy carton boxes, construct a basic monster shape. Cover the entire structure with *wide* strips or sheets of wet newspaper and paste applied with a wide paint brush. When dry, paint or spray the structure a metallic colour. Then artistically attach the acquired junk for the limbs and features of the monster!

Homemade paste: *Make homemade paste by gradually adding 125 mL (½ cup) flour to 250 mL (1 cup) cold water until you have a smooth paste. Stir over high heat until mixture thickens. Let the paste cool. Store it in a covered jar in the refrigerator. This is not as strong as store-bought paste or glue, but it works for paper and cloth and is good in an emergency, or if your child is allergic to commercial glues.*

Picture Frame

September 12 is Grandparents' Day, and nothing pleases grandparents more than being given pictures of their grandchildren, especially if the photos are in a homemade frame. Try this idea, or see if you and your child can think of other ways to make interesting frames.

Materials:
coloured magazine pages
pencil
glue or paste
cardboard
aluminum foil or coloured paper
scissors
photo

Instructions: Make the magazine pages into a thin roll by rolling them tightly from the corner of the page (use a pencil to help form the roll). After rolling a few thicknesses, glue the paper and weigh it down until the glue sets. While the glue is drying, cut a piece of cardboard about twice the size of the photograph, and cover it with foil or coloured paper.

Now trim the extra paper off the magazine-page roll. Cut it into four pieces to fit around the cardboard, and glue the pieces in place. Glue the photo to the centre of the cardboard. To make the frame stand up, attach a triangle of cardboard to the back.

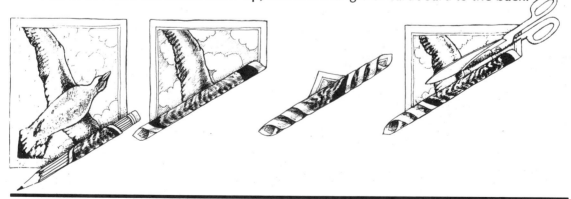

Variation: *Use a Styrofoam meat tray instead of cardboard for the back of the picture. Cover the tray with foil or paper, and use the paper rolls as an inner frame around the inside of the tray.*

Neighbourhood Map

September, which marks the beginning of school for many children, is a good time to reinforce the idea of neighbourhood. This is a long-term activity that requires lots of space.

Materials:
old shower curtain or plastic sheet
marker pens, crayons
milk cartons, small boxes
cardboard, construction paper
scissors
tape
playdough
small cushions, twigs, toy cars, toy people, etc.

Instructions: Spread out the shower curtain on the floor or table, or cut out a square as large as you can accommodate. With a marker pen or crayon, draw a map of the streets around your home, including, for example, the way to school, the park, the grocery store, and other familiar landmarks. (It's a good idea to sketch a rough map on a separate piece of paper first, to use as a guide.) Draw crosswalks and sidewalks, as well. Cover milk cartons or small boxes with coloured paper and use them as houses and buildings. Make stop signs and traffic lights out of cardboard and mount them in playdough bases. You can build up the neighbourhood over several weeks, adding trees, cars—even stuffing small cushions under the curtain to form hills! Use the map as the basis for imaginary play with other toys—to help your children learn local street names, their address, the location of traffic lights, crosswalks, neighbours' homes, and anything else of importance in your neighbourhood.

Tip: *Leftover pieces of shower curtain can be used to make bathtub puzzles. Cut out shapes, numbers, or make a simple jigsaw. When wet, the pieces will stick to the side of the bathtub!*

Leaf Mural

The leaf mural is a group project to celebrate the coming of autumn. Grade-school children can draw several trees and label them (maple, oak, willow, etc.). Then they can try to attach appropriate leaves to the parent tree.

Materials:
autumn leaves
long length of brown wrapping paper or other mural-sized paper
tape
brown marker pen or paint

Instructions: Tape the large sheet of paper to the wall. On the paper, draw the outline of a large tree with bare branches. While on an outdoor walk, collect coloured leaves from the ground. Attach the leaves to the branches with tape. Children can also tape drawings or cutouts of nuts, squirrels and birds to the tree.

Variation: *The tree outline can be used as the basis for artwork all year round, reflecting the changing seasons. In winter, add paper snowflakes or cotton balls; in spring, flower blossoms and birds' nests; in summer, green leaves and butterflies.*

Tip: *For a permanent leaf mural, wax the leaves first by pressing them between two pieces of wax paper with a warm iron.*

Autumn Peep Show

These autumn peep show landscapes will encourage children to look closely at details and small objects. Children can also use these landscapes as settings for toy animals or dinosaurs. The papier-mâché pulp is a wonderful play material that can be used to make all kinds of sculptures.

Materials:
shoe box (or other medium-sized box with lid)
aluminum foil
papier-mâché pulp (see below)
scissors
tape
tempera paint
waxed paper
coloured paper
paste or glue
marker pens or crayons
thread
twigs, dried grass and flowers, small rocks, small evergreen branches, pine cones, cotton batting, toy animals or dinosaurs, etc.

Instructions: Line the lid of the box with foil and fill it with papier-mâché pulp. Shape, pinch, poke and tunnel the pulp to make the landscape—hills, valleys, and so on. Paint the pulp while it is still wet. Then add twigs, dried grass, pebbles and small models to create an autumn landscape.

Cut one side off the box. In one end of the box, cut a peep hole about 2 cm (¾ inch) in diameter. Cover the "sides" and "top" of the box with blue paper and cotton batting to look like sky and clouds. You can even hang clouds, birds, moon, stars or sun from the top of the box with thread poked through holes in the box and then knotted. Tape a sheet of waxed paper across the open side of the box, and fit the box over the lid. Hold the box with the open side facing a light or open window, and look through the peep hole.

Papier-mâché pulp: *To make papier-mâché pulp, soak several sheets of scrunched-up newspaper in a bucket of hot water overnight, making sure the sheets are completely covered. The next morning, drain off the cold water and again cover the newspapers with hot water. Rub the soaking newspapers together until they become fibre. Squeeze the water out of the fibre. (The fibre will keep this way indefinitely.) When ready to use, add hot water and 50 mL (4 tbsp) flour to each 250 mL (1 cup) pulp and mix until the pulp is a thick, porridge-like consistency (most young children prefer working with a warm substance). Mould the pulp as desired, and paint while still wet.*

Body Paint

This textured body paint can be a special treat for a child too young to go trick-or-treating, or for a child who for some reason has to stay indoors on the big night. Children three and up can paint their own faces in the mirror or can paint one another. This soap paint keeps for a long time in a covered container, and it washes off very easily.

Materials:
soap or soap flakes
food colouring
small paintbrush
plate

Instructions: Shave the soap into small bits, or use soap flakes. Add some warm water and mix the soap into a paste. Divide it into portions on a plate, and add a different colour of food colouring to each batch. Paint designs on your child's face (keep it away from the eyes, of course!).

Variation: *This soap paint makes a nice, touchable play paint material that has many applications. Use it for finger paint (try using it on aluminum foil for a special effect). For a "stained glass" picture, dab different colours of soap paint on a piece of waxed paper. Place another piece of waxed paper on top and press lightly. Seal the edges with masking tape (or black hockey stick tape for a more dramatic effect) and hang the picture in the window to let the light shine through it.*

Foil Mask

This foil mask can be used to make life-sized moulds with plaster of Paris or papier mâché, but most young children will be content with the foil likeness. With a child's features, the "likeness" is quite subtle—for a more dramatic effect, you can cut out eye holes or have your child hold his or her mouth slightly open during the moulding, to make the lips more pronounced. Leave eyeglasses on—they make the mask even more interesting!

Materials:
piece of aluminum foil, approximately 60 cm (2 feet) long

Instructions: Fold the piece of foil in half to make it thicker, or use a single layer of heavy-duty foil. Help your child press the foil against his or her face, fitting it gently against eyes, nose and mouth. Lift it off gently.

Note: *Some young children don't like having their faces covered, but will get quite a kick out of helping you make your own mask!*

Bird and Animal Hats

The basic hat can be varied with paints, crayons or by gluing on multi-coloured paper "feathers." Try adding different-shaped ears to make strange new animals.

Materials:
light cardboard, poster board or construction paper
tape or stapler
glue
coloured paper (try using coloured pages from old magazines)
crayons or markers
scissors

Instructions: The cardboard should be about 18 cm (7 inches) wide and long enough to fit the child's head when the cardboard strip is folded at the centre. Fold and crease the strip in the centre and wrap it around your child's head. Tape or staple the ends together to fit.

Cut through both sides of the bottom of the hat, as shown. Be sure to cut a deep enough curve that the wearer's eyes will be exposed. The pointed end of the front fold will be the end of the beak or the top of the nose. Decorate the mask with coloured paper and markers.

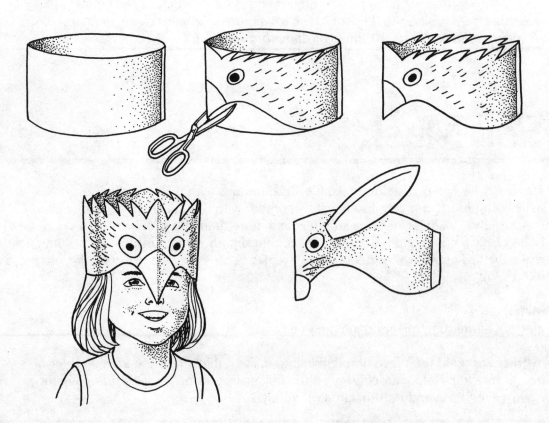

Ghost Puppets

This is a different kind of puppet—one that will glow in the dark.

Materials:
aluminum foil
glass tumbler
pencil
hand flashlight
elastic band

Instructions: Mould a piece of aluminum foil loosely over the bottom of the glass. Lift out the glass and, with a pencil, poke holes in the foil for eyes, nose and mouth. Fit the foil over the end of the flashlight and secure with an elastic band. Turn on the flashlight. Children can play with these puppets in a dark room or can enjoy their own show if they make the puppets dance in front of a window after dark.

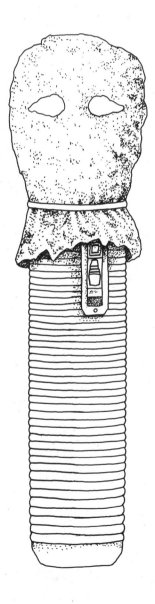

Apple Tree

November is Apple Month, and you can make a whole orchard out of these newspaper trees to celebrate. Or you can make a forest of Christmas trees, or a desert island with palm trees, or fantasy trees decorated with birds, flowers, or imaginary fruits or nuts (use feathers, glitter, buttons, baubles, and discarded jewellery). Watching the tree "grow" out of rolled up newspaper seems almost magic, but it's very easy, though it may take a bit of practice.

Materials:

newspapers   can, jar, bucket or basket
scissors   red and green paper
tape

Instructions: Use three double sheets of newspaper, or three single pages to make a smaller tree. Lay the sheets out flat, so that they are overlapping (1). Roll them up together fairly tightly from the narrow end—the finished roll should be about 5 cm (2 inches) in diameter. Hold the bottom of the roll and make three cuts into the top end (2). Space the cuts evenly around the roll. The deeper the cuts, the longer the leaves will be.

   Now make the tree grow. Holding it at the bottom, carefully pull on the inner leaves, tugging them out of the roll. You will have to rotate the inside section as you pull. The roll will telescope outward, sprouting more leaves as it grows. When it's fully grown (about twice the original length), tape the bottom so it won't come apart. Stand the tree in a can or jar, stuffing crumpled newspapers around the bottom to hold the tree upright. Cut out apples and leaves from the coloured paper and paste them on the tree.

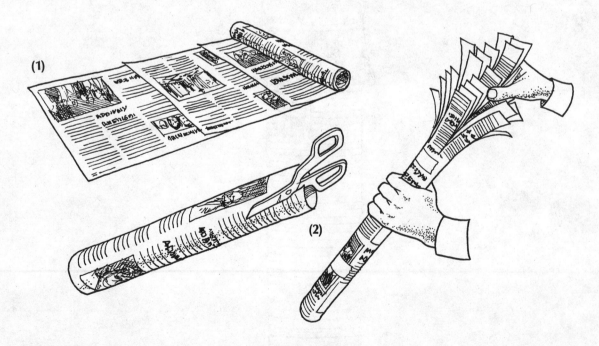

Other activities for Apple Month: *make applesauce or candy apples, visit an apple farm, have an apple-tasting or apple-bobbing party, visit an apple-doll maker.*

Making a Book

The week-long Children's Book Festival is held in November, and your school, library or local bookstore will likely be celebrating with a special event. Children love making their own books at any time of the year.

Materials:

several sheets of paper   crayons, markers, pencils
string, yarn, ribbon or stapler   magazines

Instructions: Fold several sheets of paper (at least four) in half. Punch two holes in the fold and either bind the sheets together with a piece of string or yarn, or simply staple the sheets together. Older children will enjoy writing or dictating their own stories, then illustrating them with drawings. Younger children might like to cut pictures out of magazines and paste them in. Or they might simply like to have a blank book for collecting doodles, drawings or stickers.

Variation: *Younger children especially might enjoy making folder books from one long sheet of paper folded like an accordion. They can draw or paste in photographs of different members of the family, pictures of different kinds of vehicles, foods, and so on. Or you can help them make their own shapes, colours or numbers folder. When it is finished, the folder can be hung as a frieze on the wall or in a stairwell.*

Bird Feeders

Birds like to be fed all year round, but they need to be fed the most in the winter, because that is when they can't always find the wild food they need. Once you start feeding birds, though, be sure to keep it up throughout the winter, because the birds will depend on you. The milk carton feeder may not last all winter, but a new one can be quickly made. The suet ball feeder is simple to make and provides birds with needed fat as a substitute for insects.

Milk Carton Feeder:

Materials:
2 L milk carton
scissors or paring knife
bird seed
string or wire
masking tape

Instructions: Tape the top of the milk carton shut. With a knife or scissors, cut three "windows" in the sides of the carton. Fold the sides down, then fold up a small flap for birds to perch on. Fill the bottom of the carton with bird seed. Hang the feeder outdoors, preferably in a sheltered spot.

Suet Ball Feeder:

Materials:
string
suet (available in the meat department of many grocery stores)
or cold leftover cooking fat
bird seed, bread crumbs, sunflower seeds, popcorn, oatmeal
foil or waxed paper
small mesh onion bag

Instructions: Mix the suet or fat with the seeds, crumbs, popcorn or oatmeal. Mould the mixture into a ball, wrap it in foil or newspaper and put in the freezer for a couple of hours. (It will become quite solid.) Then put the ball in the mesh bag and hang it outdoors immediately. As long as the weather stays cold, the fat and seed ball will hold its shape quite well.

Variation: *Make a pine cone feeder by using a spoon to stuff the crevices of a pine cone with peanut butter. Roll the pine cone in bird seed or oatmeal, and hang it outside.*

Tip: *Hang your bird feeder near a window and, if possible, out of the reach of squirrels. If the squirrels become a nuisance, try spreading dried corn on the ground beneath the feeder for them.*

Taffy Pull

November 25 is St. Catherine's Day. Since the seventeenth century, a taffy pull has been a French Canadian custom on this day.

Materials:
125 mL (½ cup) molasses
375 mL (1½ cups) sugar
125 mL (½ cup) water
25 mL (1½ tbsp) vinegar
1 mL (¼ tsp) cream of tartar
50 mL (3 tbsp) butter
2 mL (½ tsp) vanilla extract
waxed paper

Instructions: In a heavy saucepan, bring the molasses, sugar, water and vinegar to a boil, stirring constantly. Add the cream of tartar and boil, stirring constantly, until the mixture forms a hard ball when dropped in cold water. Blend in the butter and vanilla.

   Pour the taffy onto a buttered cookie sheet. As the candy cools around the sides, fold it in toward the centre. When the candy is cool enough to handle, pull it with your fingertips and thumbs until it is stringy and golden. Shape it into a rope or cut it into small pieces with kitchen shears. Place the pieces on waxed paper to harden.

Did You Know? *St. Catherine was the patron saint of lacemakers, spinners, carpenters and unmarried women. Fireworks and acrobatic displays have helped to celebrate St. Catherine's Day, and superstition says that you're not supposed to walk in a straight line on this day!*

Make It Snow

This is a good outdoor activity for one of those grey days in autumn when summer is over but winter hasn't quite arrived.

Materials:
flour shaker or empty spice container with shaker holes
cornstarch

Instructions: Fill the shaker with cornstarch and let your child take it outside and sprinkle anything in sight—plants, leaves, grass or stones. The cornstarch is harmless, and the first rain will wash it off.

Things to Make and Do
in the Winter

Toothpick Dreydl

The spinning top is one of the world's oldest toys. Tops have been made from nuts, stone, gourds, and even shells. In Japan, top spinners used to give performances, doing fancy tricks with their tops. During the Hanukkah holiday in December, Jewish children play games with a four-sided top called a *dreydl*. Children can have fun making and playing with tops of all kinds.

Materials:
cardboard egg carton
round toothpick
scissors
tape
markers or crayons

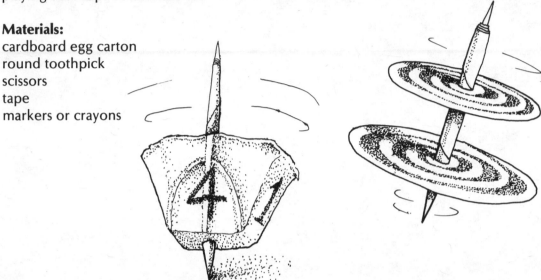

Instructions: Cut one section from a cardboard egg carton. Trim the edge so that it is even all around. Push a toothpick through the centre of the cup so that it sticks out about 5 mm (¼ inch). A little tape wrapped around the long end of the toothpick makes a better handle for spinning the top.

An actual dreydl has a different Hebrew letter on each of its four sides. Numbers or colours could be substituted. Games can be played by getting prizes or points according to which letter, number or colour is facing up when the top stops spinning.

Variation: *To make a spiral top, trace a circle on a piece of cardboard. Cut it out and mark the centre. Make a starter hole with a pin, then push a toothpick through about 1 cm (½ inch). Put a drop of glue where the toothpick goes through so it won't slip. With a marker, make a spiral line from the top's centre to its outer edge. Watch the line as the top spins!*

A double-decker top can be made by cutting a smaller circle and mounting it on the toothpick about 2 cm (1 inch) above the larger circle. Use a piece of plastic straw as a spacer between the circles. For a larger top, use a short pencil stub instead of a toothpick.

Did You Know? *Hanukkah is the Jewish holiday celebrating the festival of lights. When Judah Macabee and his followers regained control of the Temple of Jerusalem, they found only enough oil in the sacred candelabra (menorah) to last one day. Miraculously, the oil lasted for eight days. So during Hanukkah, there is feasting for eight consecutive nights, and on each night another candle is lighted.*

Chocolate Truffles

Make these chocolate truffles for holiday gifts. Older children will be able to help grate the peel and the chocolate, and even young preschoolers will enjoy the mixing, rolling, and the fun of being involved in holiday baking. These chocolates are very rich, so make them small and keep an eye on a child who is a chocolate freak. It's worth buying the more expensive imported chocolate to make these. For adult tastes, you can omit the orange peel and add ground nuts and/or a spoonful of liqueur.

Materials:
100 g (¼ lb) good quality bittersweet or semisweet chocolate
50 g (2 oz) unsalted butter
peel of ¼ orange, grated
one egg yolk
75 mL (¼ cup) cocoa or icing sugar

Instructions: Melt the chocolate and butter in the top of a double boiler. Add the grated orange peel and egg yolk and blend well. Refrigerate until chocolate is firm enough to shape (about 2 hours). Shape chocolate into balls about the size of marbles. Roll in cocoa or icing sugar and store in the refrigerator or freezer.

Newspaper Gift Wrapping

Make-it-yourself newspaper gift wrap not only saves money, but it creates an additional use for newspapers before they are eventually put out for recycling. Gifts wrapped in newspaper have a neat and crisp black-and-white look. Colour accents may be added in various ways.

Materials:
newspaper pages
markers and crayons
food colouring
tape
yarn, string or ribbon

Instructions: Use the newspaper as is, or add colour accents with markers or crayons. Try "dyeing" areas of the newspaper by wetting the paper and dropping food colouring onto the wet sections. Fold the sections over one another; the colours will penetrate the layers of paper, creating interesting patterns. The paper soon dries and can be used to wrap holiday gifts, either taped on or tied with ribbon, string or yarn.

After the gifts are unwrapped, remember to save the ribbon and other gift-tying materials to use in other crafts. If you use stickers or paper cutouts to decorate your gift wraps, be sure to remove them before putting the newspaper in the recycling box.

Candy Glass Cookies

These fancy cookies make interesting decorations for a Christmas tree and can be hung in a window where the sun can light them up. You can experiment with different shapes, too, so that these cookies can add a special touch to any holiday!

Materials:
250 mL (1 cup) margarine or butter
50 mL (¼ cup) honey
250 mL (1 cup) brown sugar
50 mL (¼ cup) water
2 mL (½ tsp) salt
750 mL (3 cups) all purpose flour
2 mL (½ tsp) baking soda
waxed paper
aluminum foil
several packages of Lifesavers, lollipops, or similar hard candy

Instructions: Mix margarine, honey and sugar together, then add water and stir until the mixture is smooth. Combine salt, flour and baking soda and stir them into the sugar mixture. Knead this dough until it feels like clay. Add more water if necessary. Wrap the dough in waxed paper and chill it in the refrigerator for 10 to 15 minutes. Meanwhile, preheat the oven to 180°C (350°F). Remove the chilled dough from the fridge and roll it into "ropes" about as thick as a pencil. (Waxed paper makes a good rolling surface.) Form the ropes into designs—angels, windows, bells, eggs, animals. Wherever the rope ends join, press them together so they won't separate when baking. Remember that the spaces between the ropes will be filled with candy "glass."

   Place your designs on a foil-covered cookie sheet and bake for 6 to 8 minutes. While they're baking, crunch the candy into bits, keeping each colour separate. Take the cookies out of the oven, let them cool, and then fill the spaces in each design with a layer of coloured candy. Bake them some more until the candy melts, about 6 minutes. Remove them from the oven, let them cool, and peel them off the foil. Now you can hang up your decorations . . . or eat them!

Piñata

Real piñatas are *very* hard to break, so here's an idea for a homemade version that is easier to burst open. If not too many kids are involved, each one can use a rolled up newspaper instead of a stick, and everyone can try to hit the piñata at the same time (as long as everyone is careful not to hit everyone else!).

Materials:
tissue paper
tape
scissors
markers
coloured paper
paste or glue
candies and other treats to fill the piñata
string

Instructions: Fold a sheet of tissue paper in half and tape the sides together to form a loose bag. By cutting or folding the corners, you can form a shape that looks like an animal. Decorate the piñata with markers or shapes cut out of coloured paper. Crumple up some small pieces of tissue and stuff them inside the piñata to fill it out. There will still be plenty of room to add candies and small treats. Paste or glue the top of the piñata closed, and it's ready to hang.

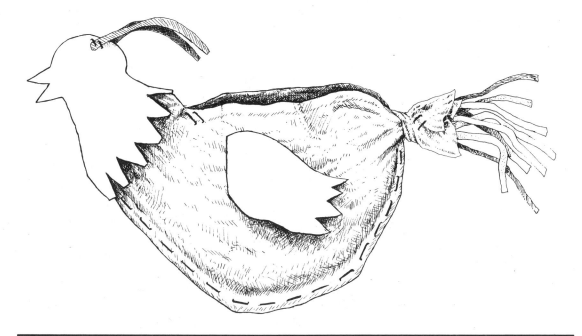

Did You Know? *The breaking of the piñata is part of the Christmas celebration in Mexico. Sometimes the piñata is an earthenware jug decorated and filled with candies or small gifts. Other piñatas are made of papier mâché in the shape of a donkey or other animal. The piñata is hung from a string outdoors or indoors. A child is blindfolded and given three chances to swing at the piñata with a stick. Each child tries in turn until the piñata is finally broken, and all the goodies are shared.*

Inkblot Giftwrap

Children will love making inkblot pictures on plain paper or construction paper, and inkblot artwork also makes attractive giftwrap. When wrapping gifts, use a double or triple thickness of newspaper to prevent tearing.

Materials:
sheets of newspaper
thick tempera paint
empty squeeze container (detergent, hand lotion, etc.)

Instructions: Fill the squeeze container with thick paint. Open up a sheet of newspaper. Squeeze paint down the centre fold of the sheet (any errant drips and drizzles make it even more interesting). Fold the sheet of paper in half. Open it up and let the paint dry. Ask your child to imagine what the shapes look like, and to give careful thought to whose gift should be wrapped in which giftwrap.

What's in the Stocking?

Here's a guessing game for two or more to play while waiting to hang up stockings on Christmas Eve. Use a Christmas stocking or a regular sock.

Materials:
a large sock or stocking
many small objects such as a marble, small toy, clothespin, comb, toothbrush

Instructions: One player (or parent) puts several items in a sock. The sock is then passed around, with each player trying to guess what's inside by feeling the objects through the sock.

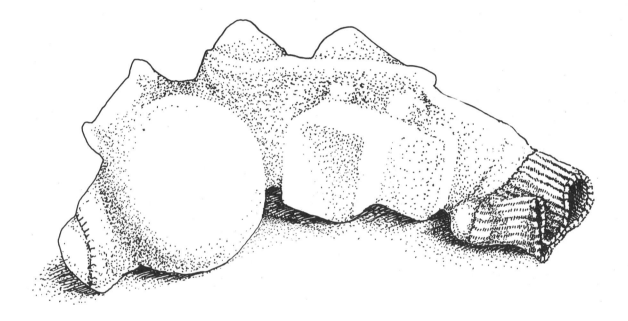

Variations: *Hunt outdoors for larger objects such as pine cones, rocks, twigs or pieces of bark. Place objects under a towel or in a pillowcase, and try to guess by feeling what they are. Slightly older children can play an identification game using the Christmas nut bowl. Blindfold a child and let him or her try to name the nuts by feeling the texture and shape of the shells. Start with a few nuts and gradually build up to several different kinds.*

Fingerprint Pictures

January 6 is the birthday of the famous detective, Sherlock Holmes. As a change from painting and finger painting, try airy fingerprint artwork. Older children will discover that everyone's fingerprints are different, and if they have an old stamp pad, they can "collect" friends' fingerprints and examine them under a magnifying glass. Younger preschoolers will love simply making handprint and footprint collages on a discarded white sheet or tablecloth (very small fingers won't always leave identifiable "prints").

Materials:
paper towels
plate
thick tempera paint
paper

Instructions: Lay several layers of paper towel on the plate. Let a thick solution of tempera paint soak into it. Press a finger into the towel and then onto the paper (if there's too much paint the first time, make a second or third print without using any more paint). Make a collage of fingerprints, handprints or footprints. Try making a fingerprint "chain," or use different colours for hands, feet and fingers. The fingerprints can also be used as the basis for artwork—add lines to make animals, people, flowers—almost anything!

Variation: *Try making pictures based on hand tracings or prints. Help your child trace his or her hand with the thumb and fingers in different positions. Decide what the tracing looks like, then finish the picture. Try turning the tracing sideways or even upside-down for a different perspective. This is a good activity for children who can't think of what to draw.*

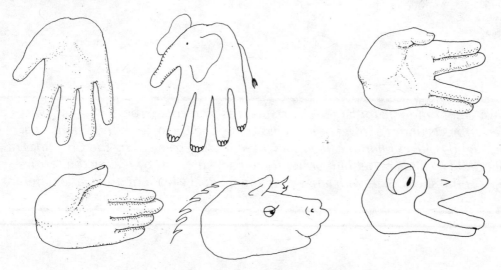

Tip: *For really "professional" prints, slowly roll the fingertip onto the paper.*

Did You Know? *Everyone's toe prints, elbow prints and palm prints are all completely different.*

Snowy Jars

There are many ways to make the "snow" for these jars. The tapioca in this version looks like real snow, but the mixture must be prepared a day ahead. If you don't have time for this, cut foil into tiny pieces and put them in water (make the pieces quite small — they will look bigger when they are in the water). The shiny bits look especially magical in sunlight. Or try coconut flakes in water, or crushed white egg shells (remove the membrane first) in a jar of mineral oil.

Materials:
5 mL (1 tsp) instant tapioca
cold water
small jar (e.g., baby-food jar)
water-resistant glue
small figurines, clean stones, dried playdough creatures, etc.

Instructions: In a clean glass or jar, mix 250 mL (1 cup) cold water with the tapioca. Let the mixture sit overnight, or up to two days. Skim any powdery scum off the surface (most of the tapioca will sink to the bottom). Strain the mixture through a strainer and rinse with cold water.

Glue a figurine, stones, etc., onto the inside bottom of the jar. Let dry.

Put the tapioca in the strainer in the jar and fill with clean cold water. Screw on the jar lid tightly.

Whenever you want it to snow, turn the jar upside down!

Snow Scenes

This is another way to make snow scene pictures. Older children can draw a winter scene first with chalk and then paste popcorn or styrofoam onto the snowy areas.

Materials:
paste or glue
dark-coloured construction paper
leftover popcorn, or Styrofoam peanuts or pebbles

Instructions: Make a shape or design with the paste on the construction paper. Sprinkle popcorn or Styrofoam bits onto the paste. If very fine snow is desired, for a blizzard scene or 3-dimensional snow bank, you can grate the Styrofoam with a kitchen grater.

Snow Painting

You can also bring snow inside for this activity. Lay it on a chilled cookie sheet, and put the finished design in the freezer to show others later on.

Materials:
snow
empty squeeze bottle
thin tempera paint or water with food colouring added

Instructions: Fill a squeeze bottle with paint. Squeeze the paint onto the snow, either outside or inside, to make designs and pictures.

Draft Snake

Even young children can make this simple draft stopper out of an old pair of tights. Older children can decorate the finished snake by gluing or sewing on button eyes, wool tongue and other decorations. Sawdust or wood chips can also be used as stuffing materials, but they are messier than the beans.

Place the snake on a drafty windowsill or at the bottom of a leaky door at night.

Materials:
old pair of tights
elastic band
scissors
buttons, felt pieces, ribbons, wool
dried beans (kidney beans or other large beans are the easiest to handle)

Instructions: Cut both legs off the tights. Carefully insert one leg inside the other to make a double thickness (this should take care of the odd hole or tear, but check to make sure there are no leaks). Stuff the leg loosely with dried beans. Secure the end tightly with an elastic band.

If you wish, decorate the snake with wool, ribbon and felt scraps.

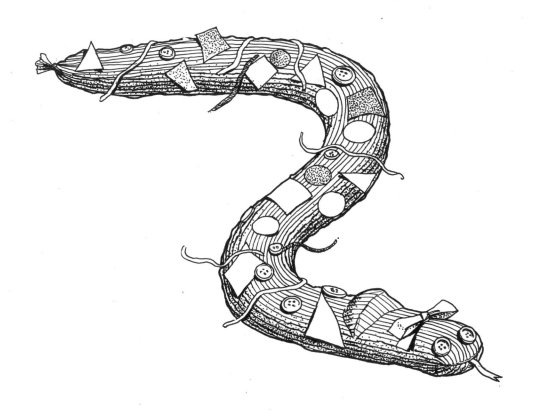

Indoor Snowman

During February, winter carnivals take place throughout the country. You can make this indoor snowman to look like Bonhomme, the mascot of the Quebec Winter Carnival (he wears a red toque and belt—*ceinture fléchée*), or just make a regular snowman.

Materials:
newspaper
3 white pillowcases
toothpicks
carrot, prunes, buttons, etc.
scarf
hat

Instructions: Scrunch up individual sheets of newspaper and stuff the three pillowcases. Tie the top and bottom corners of each pillowcase together to form large balls. Stack the pillowcases to make a snowman. For eyes, nose, mouth and buttons, attach a carrot, prunes and buttons to the snowman with toothpicks. Wrap a scarf around the snowman's neck and put an old hat on his head.

Make a Moustache

A moustache contest is a traditional event of the Quebec Winter Carnival, the largest winter carnival in the world. Kids can have fun making silly moustaches and beards for dressup play. The moustache may give children ideas for dressing up or talking in a strange voice.

Materials:
yarn, cotton batting, feathers, string, leaves, twine, grass, coloured paper, Easter basket straw, or any other appropriate material
tape
makeup (see Soap Paint on page 17)
marker pens
charcoal

Instructions: Cut a moustache shape out of a piece of coloured paper. Decorate it with marker pens, string, yarn, cotton batting, or whatever you have gathered. Use tape or thick, wet soap to attach the moustache. Or paint a moustache shape using makeup or charcoal.

Tip: *If you have no charcoal, burn the end of a cork with a match for a homemade substitute.*

Dragon Dressup

Dragons are interesting storybook creatures, and Chinese dragons are the fanciest of all! During Chinese New Year and Spring Festival celebrations, huge, long dragons with many legs parade up the street, opening their big mouths to snap up good luck gifts from the people along the way. A group of kids can make their own dragon.

Materials:
cardboard box or large paper bag
newspapers, coloured paper, paper streamers
markers
tape
scissors
blanket, tablecloth or sheet

Instructions: To make the head, use a cardboard box or a large paper bag. This will be worn by the front person in the dragon. Cut a hole to see through. If a box is used, cut off all but one flap of the box. The remaining flap is the jaw of the dragon, and can be wiggled up and down as the dragon moves. Everyone can join in decorating the head with ears, horns, teeth, whiskers and scales (metallic caps from deodorant and cosmetic containers make good bulging dragon eyes). Paper streamers can be taped to the blanket "body." The more fluttery, wavey, wiggley pieces there are, the better the dragon looks!

When all is ready, choose one person to be the first to hold or wear the head. The others form the body, covered by the sheet or blanket. Then it's time to start the dragon parade!

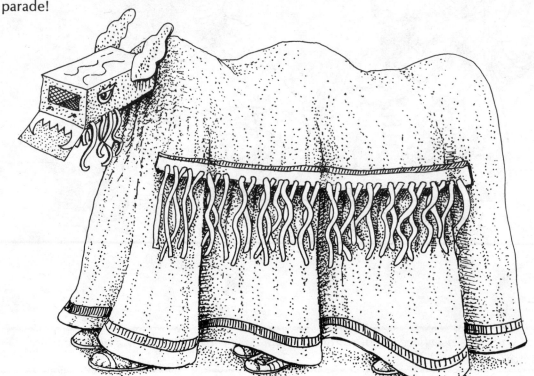

Victorian Valentine

For an unusual valentine, try making this old-fashioned Victorian valentine that says, "My heart is in your hands!"

Materials:
coloured paper
pencil
scissors
paste or glue
marker pens or crayons
doilies, cotton batting, foil, glitter, etc.

Instructions: Fold a piece of paper (at least 20 cm or 8 inches square) in half. With a pencil, trace the child's open hand, keeping the baby finger lined up with the fold (see diagram). Cut out the hand outline. Cut out a heart shape that is about the size of the palms of the hands. Paste the heart in the centre of the open hands. Decorate the valentine with small hearts, doilies, foil, or whatever you have chosen, and/or print a message in the middle of the heart.

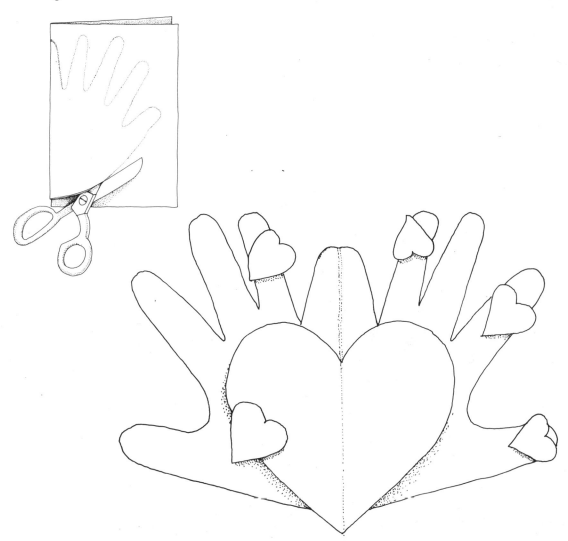

Ring Toss Game

This is an adaptation of a game that Indian and Inuit children have played for centuries.

Materials:
paper towel tube
string
mason jar lid or rubber ring, empty masking tape spool or ring made from a sheet of
newspaper rolled up and stapled or taped together
newspaper

Instructions: Punch a hole in one end of the paper towel tube and thread a piece of
string approximately 60 cm (2 ft) long through the hole. Knot the string. Tie the ring to
the other end of the string. To play, hold the end of the paper towel tube in one hand.
Fling the ring into the air and try to catch it on the tube.

 To make the game easier, shorten the length of the string. To make the game more
difficult, make the string longer and thread it through several rings. Tie the string to the
final ring.

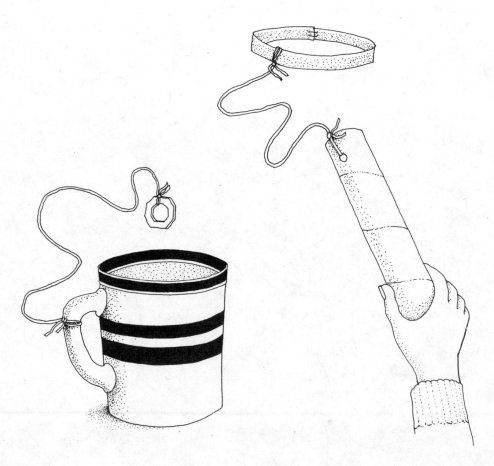

Variation: *Younger children can tie a washer to a short length of string attached to a
plastic or tin cup handle and then try to flip the washer into the cup.*

Totem Pole

Here's a good Heritage Day activity for February. West coast Indians carved totem poles from huge trees. The totem poles usually depicted animal shapes and figures. Using these cardboard buildups, children can build totem poles and all sorts of constructions, towers and monsters.

Materials:
scissors
toilet paper rolls and paper towel rolls
flat cardboard (such as shirt cardboard)
milk cartons and small boxes
crayons or marker pens

Instructions: Prepare the cardboard rolls by cutting slits in each end: four slits about 2 cm (1 inch) deep opposite one another, as shown (1). Cut the cardboard into rectangles about 4 cm by 8 cm (1½ inches by 3 inches). Cut slits 1 cm (½ inch) deep into each end and into the middle (2). Cut milk cartons in half. Then cut out their bottoms to make hollow squares (3).

Fit the different pieces together and experiment with different combinations. Cardboard rectangles can join rolls together at right angles. Have a contest to see who can join the most pieces together before it all falls apart. Decorate the construction with crayons or marker pens.

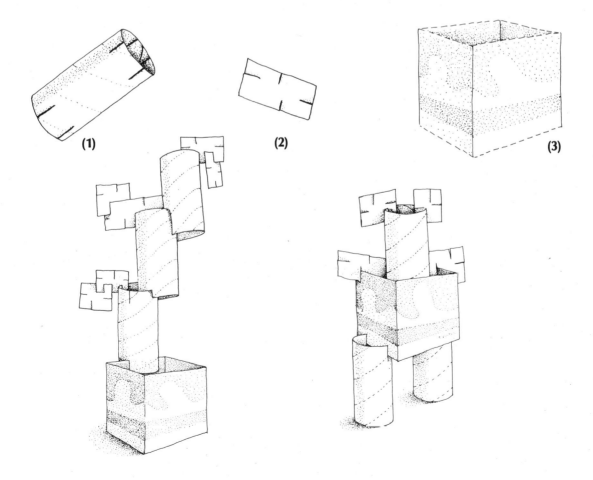

(1)   (2)   (3)

Things to Make and Do in the Spring

Fancy Pancakes

Shrove Tuesday is Pancake Day. You can use any ready-mixed or homemade pancake batter to make pancakes, but this recipe makes quite a thick batter and the pancakes will hold their shape.

Materials:
300 mL (1¼ cups) sifted all-purpose flour
12 mL (2½ tsp) baking powder
50 mL (3 tbsp) sugar
2 mL (½ tsp) salt
50 mL (3 tbsp) vegetable oil
1 egg
250 mL (1 cup) milk

Instructions: Oil a frying pan and preheat to medium-high heat. Sift the dry ingredients together, then add the remaining ingredients, and stir everything together lightly (batter will be lumpy). Drop spoonfuls of batter into the frying pan. Make pancakes with big mouse ears, pancakes that look like snowmen, etc. Flip pancakes when the tops have lost their sheen.

Styrofoam Tray Prints

Spring is a good time to think about recycling and conservation.
   Save the Styrofoam trays that fresh meats are sold on. They are useful for many crafts. Making prints is a colourful way of using these trays.

Materials:
Styrofoam trays
pencil or ballpoint pen
scissors
paint brush
tempera paint or finger paint
paper

Instructions: On the flat bottom of the tray, draw a design or a simple picture with the pen or pencil. Press fairly hard. This indents the foam material and will be the white part of your print. Cut the tray to a smaller size if you think it will be easier to handle. Cover the design and surrounding area with an even layer of paint. Press it onto a sheet of paper, being careful not to slide the tray, as this will smudge the design.

Variation: *Print one design over another in different colours, or paint two or three colours on different sections of the design at the same time.*

Stuffed Paper Animals

These stuffed animal cutouts can be hung from the ceiling or in a window. Make a whole menagerie to celebrate National Wildlife Week in early April!

Materials:
large sheets of paper
paints or marker pens
stapler
newspaper

Instructions: Draw a large outline of an animal on a piece of paper—about 60 cm (2 feet) square. Paint or decorate the animal, then cut it out through two thicknesses of paper. Staple around the outline leaving one open side (most three-year-olds can handle a hand stapler safely). Stuff the animal with crumpled newspapers and staple the remaining side closed.

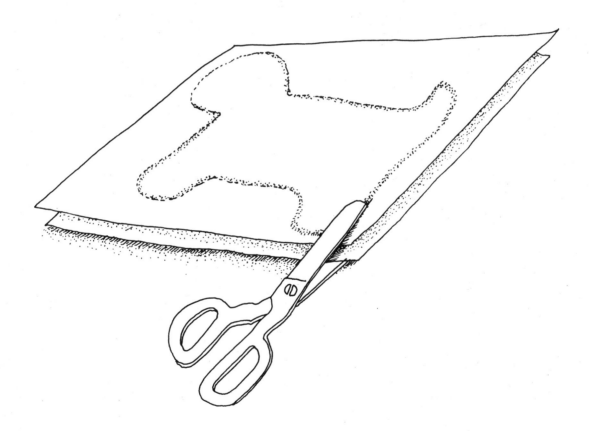

Balancing Bird

On a balmy spring day, watch and listen for birds returning north. Then you can make a fancy balancing bird that will spin around if you put it near an open window. Older children might be interested in trying to balance the bird without the coins, to learn a bit about balance points.

Materials:

paper	pencil
lightweight cardboard	cork
crayons or paints	bottle
scissors	needle or toothpick
two pennies	transparent tape

Instructions: Fold the paper in half and draw half a bird shape on the fold, as shown (or you could draw the shape of a plane or butterfly). Cut out the shape through both layers of paper, open it flat, place it on a piece of cardboard and trace it. Then colour the bird and cut it out. Tape a penny underneath the end of each wing. Put the cork in the top of the bottle and push the needle or toothpick into the top of the cork. Balance the bird on the tip of the needle.

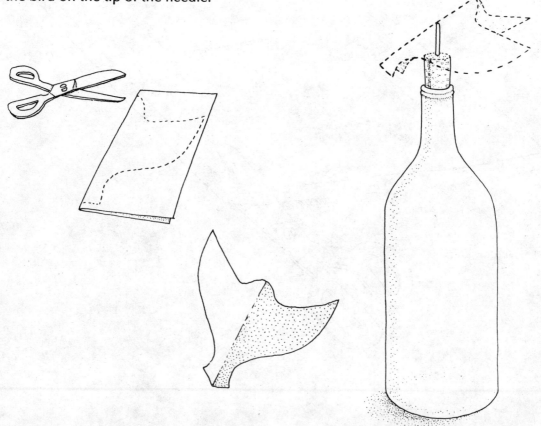

Variation: *Younger children can make a simpler balancing bird. On a piece of paper, draw a bird shape (this can be done freehand). Colour the bird, then cut it out. Tape a coin to the underside of the bird's head. Watch the bird balance by resting the coin on the tip of your finger, the rim of a cup or bowl or the edge of a table.*

Smelly Jars

Spring is a good time of year to encourage children to develop their sense of smell. Try this before taking a walk on a spring day, when the smells of the earth, evergreens and spring flowers are most noticeable.

Materials:
several large orange juice cans
aluminum foil
pencil
elastic bands
things to smell, such as an onion, lemon, coffee grounds, vinegar, banana, spices and herbs (ginger, cinnamon, mint, oregano)

Instructions: Help your child fill each can with a different item—slice the onion and lemon (add a bit of grated peel to the lemon as well). Cover each can with a piece of aluminum foil and fasten with an elastic band. Punch holes in the top of the foil. Mix up the cans and smell them. Ask your child to try to identify the contents or to describe the various odours.

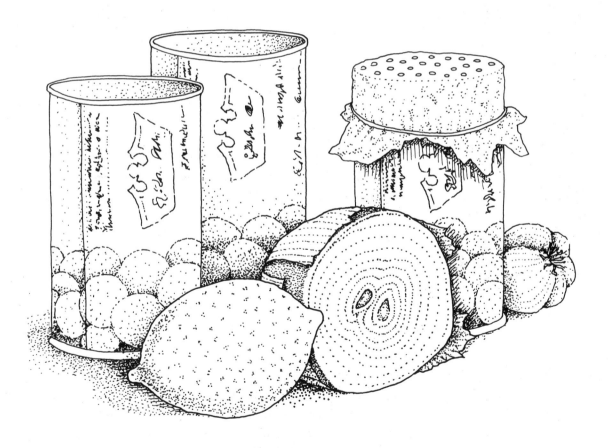

Bird Nesting Rack

Spring is the time when birds make their nests. You can help them by making a rack filled with nesting materials.

Materials:
piece of wire mesh, or large mesh fruit or onion bag
string
nails
bird nesting materials—yarn, paper strips, straw, dried grass, thread, strips of cloth, cotton batting, small twigs, roots

Instructions: Stick the nesting materials through the holes in the mesh. Hang the rack outdoors from a low tree branch and see whether the birds come shopping for nesting materials.

Did you ever wonder how a bird, without fingers or hands, is able to make a soft, comfortable nest for itself and its babies? How does the bird manage to weave the found materials together? How does the nest stay in position on the branch, ledge or window sill? For the fun of it, collect mud, twigs, dried grass and other nesting materials, and try to make a bird's nest.

Easter Egg Printing

There are many ways to colour and decorate Easter eggs, but printing on eggs with a potato gives eggs quite a different look.

Materials:
hard-boiled eggs
small potato
small paring knife
paper towel
egg dye, food colouring
plate

Instructions: Cut the potato lengthwise into a stick that is comfortable to handle. Carve one end into a small, simple design, such as a diamond or circle. To make an inkpad, fold the piece of paper towel into four layers and place it on the plate. Put several drops of full-strength egg dye or food colouring on the paper towel. Press the potato into the colour, then print the design on the eggs. You can print a deep colour onto an egg that has been dyed a pale colour.

Bat and Ball

Swatting this paper ball around can be a great way to let off steam on a rainy spring day. For younger children, make the bat shorter and the ball a little bigger, or use a balloon instead of a ball.

Materials:
newspaper
small paper or plastic bag
masking tape

Instructions: To make the ball, tear a sheet of newspaper into pieces and scrunch them up. Stuff the newspaper into the bag and wrap tape around it, forming it into a ball.

   To make the bat, lay about twelve sheets of newspaper together and fold in half. Tightly roll the newspaper lengthwise, starting at the folded edge, and tape the roll together.

Variation: *Try balancing the ball on the end of a toilet paper roll "tee" and "drive" the ball into an armchair target with the newspaper "golf club." Or try to "putt" the ball along the floor into a wastebasket or box lying on its side.*

Spring Baskets

The homemade paper bag basket can be filled with flowers for a Mother's Day gift. The egg carton can be used to carry Easter eggs.

Paper Bag Basket:

Materials:

small paper bag (lunch bag size) coloured paper
scissors tape or glue

Instructions: Cut off the top part of the paper bag so that the bag is about 7 cm (3 inches) deep. Fold the bag once so that the bottom and top are lined up (1). Cut four slits through the fold, about 2 cm (1 inch) deep. Space them so that the outside slits cut through the inner creases of the sides of the bag (2). Open the bag—there should be twelve slits in all. Cut long strips of coloured paper and weave them in and out of the slits (two or more strips may have to be glued together to go all the way around the basket). Use another strip for the basket handle (3).

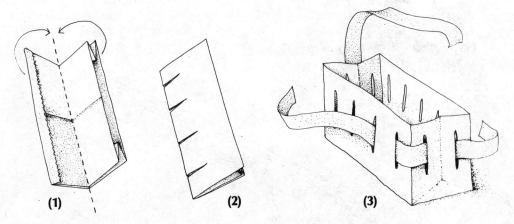

(1) (2) (3)

Egg Carton Basket:

Materials:

cardboard
egg carton
scissors
coloured paper
coloured wool
hairpin, plastic twist tie or pipe cleaner
tape

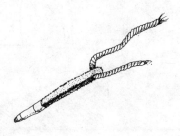

Instructions: Cut the bottom of the egg carton in half, crosswise. Attach a strip of coloured paper to each end for a handle. Punch holes along the rim between each cup. Make a "needle" out of a hairpin, plastic twist tie or bent pipe cleaner (tape the ends together as shown). Thread wool in and out of the holes. Thread around the rim twice, going in opposite directions, so that the wool shows on the outside between every hole. The handle can be threaded with wool, too.

Paper Bag Kite

In May, the Japanese celebrate Children's Day by flying kites of all shapes and sizes. Some look like fish or birds, while others are diamond-shaped. There are box kites, too—some big enough to lift a person into the air. A simple tube kite, similar to an Oriental fish kite, can be made from a paper bag.

Materials:
medium-sized paper bag
construction paper
tape or glue
markers or crayons
string
tissue paper

Instructions: Cut the bottom off the bag, making it into a tube. Decorate the bag with markers or crayons. To make the bag hold its tubular shape, cut a strip of construction paper about three fingers wide, and tape or glue it around one open end of the bag. Cut three pieces of string the length of the bag. Attach them, evenly spaced, around the reinforced end of the bag. Tie the free ends together and attach a long pull-string to this knot.

A tail helps a kite to balance. To make one, cut a piece of string about two and a half times the length of the kite. Make several bow-shaped twists of tissue paper 5 cm (2 inches) long, and tie them into the string. Attach the tail to the end of the kite that is not reinforced with the paper strip.

If there's no wind to make the kite fly, tie the kite string to a stick and twirl it around above your head. In a wide open space free of traffic and overhead wires or branches, try running with it to make it rise into the air!

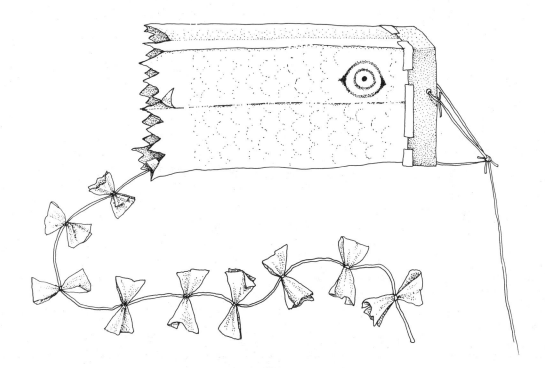

Origami House

Origami is an intricate art that is too exacting for young preschoolers, but older children may enjoy making this simple origami house. Try using different sizes of paper.

Materials:
piece of square paper, preferably coloured
marker pens or crayons

Instructions: Fold the paper in half (1), then into quarters (2). Unfold the paper once (3). Fold both sides into the middle crease (4), then unfold them again (5). Fold the top corners down to the outside creases (6), then open the corners up to make a squash fold (7). Now colour the house and draw doors, windows, and whatever else strikes the imagination (8).

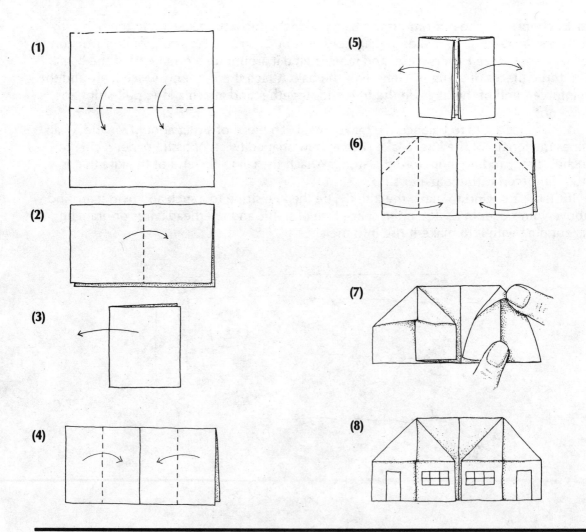

Tip: *Paper folding requires manual dexterity to make neat folds, but it also requires the ability to read diagrams. Help your child learn how to follow the instructional diagrams by explaining the meaning of the dotted lines, arrows and shaded and unshaded areas. Often, kids are better at reading diagrams than grownups!*

Napkin Rings

Make these napkin rings as a Mother's Day gift or as an eco-project for Earth Day (April 22) to encourage the use of cloth napkins instead of throwaway paper ones. Old wrapping paper rolls are usually sturdier than toilet paper or paper towel rolls, but they are more difficult to cut.

For the ultimate use of recycled materials, tear old cotton print fabric into long strips and use these to wrap around the rolls. A strip of fabric about 2.5 cm (1 inch) wide and 1 metre (3 feet) long should be enough to cover one ring.

Materials:
toilet paper or paper towel rolls, or old wrapping paper rolls
scissors
strip of colourful fabric, at least 1 metre (3 feet) long
tape or stapler

Instructions: Cut the cardboard rolls into 4 cm (1½-inch) lengths. If you are using thin cardboard, use two sections for each ring (cut a slit in one, slip it inside the other and tape it in place as reinforcement).

Staple, tape or tie one end of fabric onto the ring. Wrap the wool or fabric strips around the ring until it is covered. Staple or tie the ends in place.

Hairy Cup Dolls

Celebrate spring by making these grass-haired dolls. This is a good school project to start just before spring break—by the time the children return to school, the grass should have sprouted.

Materials:
grass seed, radish seed or bird seed
Styrofoam cup
marker pens
water
cotton batting
plastic bag (sandwich size)
twist tie

Instructions: Using marker pens, draw a face on the side of the Styrofoam cup. Fill the cup with wet cotton batting, packing it down quite firmly. Sprinkle a spoonful of grass seed on the cotton. Place the cup in a plastic bag and seal with a twist tie. Place the cup in indirect sunlight—the grass "hair" should sprout within a week. When the grass is about 3 cm (1 inch) long, remove the plastic bag and keep the cotton moist.

Variation: *You can also plant a miniature "lawn" in potting soil in a cake pan, or a "field" of leaf lettuce.*

Things to Make and Do in the Summer

Recipe Card Holder

A good Father's Day gift. You can use plastic forks if necessary.

Materials:
old fork, preferably luncheon or dessert size
newspaper
masking tape
coloured paper, paint, stickers for decorations
tape or glue

Instructions: Fold a double sheet of newspaper in half lengthwise. Keep folding until you have a folded strip about 7.5 cm (3 inches) wide (the taller your fork, the wider the strip should be). Roll up the strip fairly tightly to make a cylinder shape. Tape the ends securely.

   Decorate the outside of the roll with coloured paper, paint, stickers or other decorations.

   Stand the roll up and stick the handle of a fork in the top. The fork will hold a recipe card or placecard.

Sundial

Celebrate the first day of summer by making a sundial. Children will have fun marking their own special times of day.

Materials:

cardboard or stiff paper

paper plate, 20 to 25 cm (8 to 10 inches) wide

tape

glue

scissors

Instructions: To make the base of the sundial, cut a circle from a piece of cardboard or cut the rim from a paper plate, leaving the flat, round inner surface. Next, cut a triangle from the stiff paper or cardboard. Make the bottom of the triangle one-half the diameter of the base circle. Make the height of the triangle one-half its bottom measurement. This triangle is called the "hand" of the sundial, and it makes the shadow that tells the time. To attach it to the base, fold over about 1 cm (½ inch) along its bottom edge. This makes a tab to glue or tape the triangle to the base. Attach the triangle to the centre of the base as shown.

Place the sundial by a window that faces south, with the low end of the triangle toward the window. Try not to move it once it's in place. Notice the line of shadow made by the hand. It will be shortest and skinniest at noon. Make a mark along the shadow at different times of day. Mark meal times, TV show times, nap time and other special times of the day.

Tip: *For an outdoor sundial, mark the circle on a wide piece of wood, and cut the hand from a piece of aluminum from a throw-away food container. For an even simpler outdoor version, plant a large straight stick or pole in the middle of the backyard, or where there is plenty of open space. Mark the hours or special times around the pole with smaller sticks or pegs.*

Make a Flag

Each country's flag has colours and designs that have a certain meaning, and children can design their own flags using colours and images that are special to them.

Materials:
paper or cloth
crayons, markers or pictures from magazines
glue or tape
pencils, pipe cleaners, sticks or drinking straws for flag staffs

Instructions: Cut a rectangular, square or triangular shape out of the paper or cloth. This will be the flag. Draw a design on both sides of the flag using crayons, markers or pictures cut from magazines. A favourite food, toy, pet, sport or colour could be the basis of the design. Attach the flag to its flag staff with tape or glue. Flags can be put on bicycles and tricycles, on a jacket or shirt, or on a window.

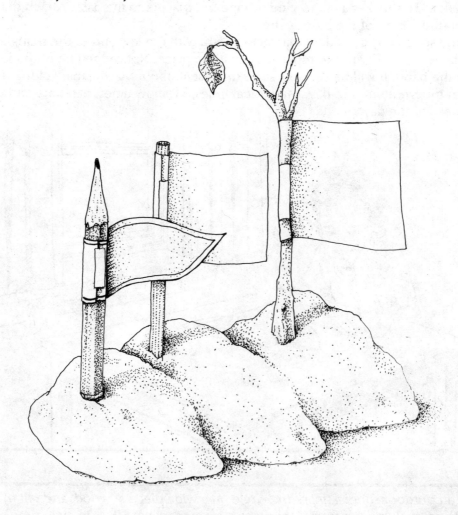

Variations: *Try making several flags and mounting them in individual playdough stands or in one large stand. For playdough recipes, refer to page 63.*

Water Painting

This is a warm-weather activity that can keep small children occupied for hours.

Materials:
bucket full of water
paint brushes, plant sprayer, empty detergent container, etc.

Instructions: Using paint brushes, sprayer or squeeze bottles, "paint" water pictures or designs on the side of the house, garage door, fence or sidewalk. Try "painting" metal objects such as wheelbarrows, watering cans or railings.

Bubble Play

You can also use this mixture to make giant bubbles outdoors, but for young children this indoor version is more manageable, and it makes a good rainy-day activity. The glycerin isn't essential, but it will make the bubbles stronger and bigger.

Two children can place themselves at either end of the baking sheet and have a race to see whose bubbles can reach the middle of the tray first!

Materials:
50 mL (¼ cup) liquid dishwashing detergent
15 to 60 mL (2 to 4 tbsp) glycerin
250 mL (1 cup) water

large baking sheet, with rim
plastic straw or turkey baster, etc.

Instructions: In a measuring cup, combine the detergent, glycerin and water.

Wet the baking sheet with water. Pour in the bubble mixture. Place one end of the straw in the bubble mixture and blow gently to make bubbles on the sheet, or place the end of the turkey baster in the mixture and squeeze the rubber bulb. See how big your bubbles can be. Try building bubbles on top of bubbles, or making little bubbles inside big ones.

Blotty Designs

Here's a good indoor activity that requires few materials and little preparation. When dry, these designs can be used as party place mats, as backgrounds for photos or magazine cutouts or as wall decorations.

Materials:
several colours of food colouring
cups or saucers

newsprint, paper towels or cloth
newspaper

Instructions: Make several strong mixtures of food colouring and water, with a different colour in each container. Fold the paper or cloth a few times in a random way so that there are three or four corners sticking out. Dip each corner in a different colour, and lay out on sheets of newspaper to dry. If the paper or cloth doesn't soak up the colour easily, moisten the material first, and squeeze the water out until it's just damp.

Paper Blowing Race

Here's a simple rainy day game for the cottage, which requires few materials and little preparation. If you have some string, paper and tape, an instant game can be set up for one person or for a whole party.

Materials:
paper
string
tape
two chairs

Instructions: Cut two 13 cm (5 inch) squares out of the paper. Fold each piece into a cone, making sure that there is a small opening at the tip of each cone. Place the chairs about 2 metres (6 feet) apart. Pass a piece of string through the cone and tie each end to a chair, stretching it tightly. Do the same with a second piece of string. Usually, the two lengths of string may be tied side-by-side to each pair of chairs. Position the cone on the string near one chair. Make the cone move to the other end of the string by blowing into the cone. Play in teams or alone.

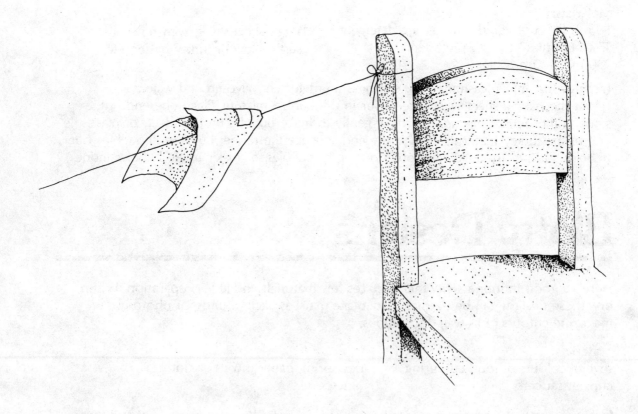

Volcano

Your children may not remember the summer that Mount St. Helen's erupted, but here's a way to show them what a volcano looks like. This activity makes a bit of a mess and the effect is short-lived, but children won't want you to stop. Spread lots of newspaper and be prepared to go through a whole bottle of vinegar!

Materials:

newspapers	mug or jar
light cardboard	powdered tempera paint
masking tape	baking soda
scissors	white vinegar
paper cup	spoon

Instructions: Cover the kitchen table or a spot on the floor with several layers of newspaper for easy cleanup. Shape a piece of cardboard approximately 50 cm by 20 cm (20 inches by 8 inches) into a cone and fasten with masking tape. Trim the bottom so that the cone is level. The hole in the top of the cone should be about 3 cm (1 inch) in diameter.

In the paper cup, put 50 mL (3 tbsp) baking soda and 5 mL (1 tsp) tempera paint. Balance the paper cup on top of an inverted jar or mug so that the cone just fits over the top of the cup. Pour 50 mL (3 tbsp) vinegar through the hole in the cone and watch the volcano erupt. When the fizzle has died down, try adding a different colour of paint, then more vinegar!

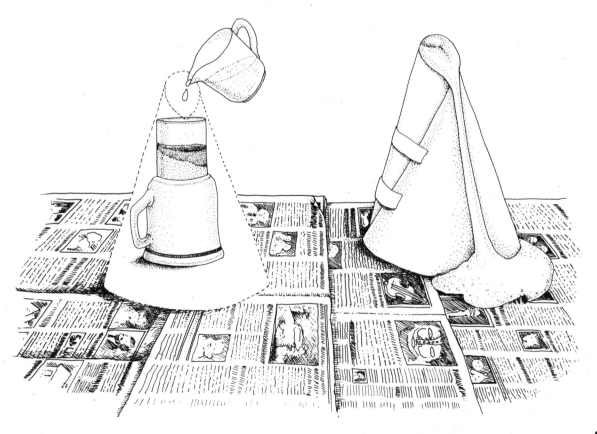

Egg Carton Toss Game

This is another easy-to-make indoor activity that's good for a rainy summer day.

Materials:
egg carton
coin, button or similar object for a "tosser"
marker pen

Instructions: Cut the top off an egg carton. Cut the bottom of the egg carton in two, crosswise, so that you have two rows of three cups each. Write a number from 1 to 6 in any order in each cup. Decide how many tosses each player may have. Toss a coin or button toward the carton, trying each time to make it land in the highest numbered cup.

Variation: *Make a list of six different things a player must do, one for each number. The number of the cup the tosser lands in decides which action the player will do. Suggestions for actions: sing a song; say the alphabet as fast as you can; pat your head and rub your tummy at the same time; go into the kitchen and turn around three times, then come back; do a peacock imitation; take thirty "giant" steps around the room; do ten "scissor jumps," etc.*

Star Gazing

Between August 10 and August 13, there is a meteor shower in the northern sky, which makes this a good time for star gazing and watching for shooting stars. Star gazing is especially impressive if you live in the country or are spending time at the beach or a summer cottage.

Materials:
blanket, sleeping bag, or ground sheet

Instructions: After dark on a clear night, go outside and wrap up in a blanket or ground sheet to keep warm. Lie on your back on the beach, the dock or in the middle of the yard. Try to choose a spot where there are no trees or buildings blocking your side vision. Listen to the summer sounds and gaze up at the sky. Soon you'll feel as if you're almost floating in the middle of space.

Variation: *Star gazing can be an even more mind-boggling experience in the middle of winter, when sounds are muffled and the air is crisp and clear. Bundle up and take a sleeping bag to keep warm!*

62

Playdough

The cooked playdough takes longer to make than the "raw" type, but your child can help mix and measure the ingredients, and perhaps make up a cooking song to pass the time while the mixture is cooking. The results are worth the waiting, as the cooked playdough is more workable than the uncooked version. Both kinds will keep indefinitely if stored in a plastic bag or container in the refrigerator.

Raw playdough

Materials:
500 mL (2 cups) flour
15 mL (1 tbsp) oil
250 mL (1 cup) salt
175 to 250 mL (¾ to 1 cup) water
food colouring

Instructions: Combine the dry ingredients in a bowl. In a measuring cup, combine the water and food colouring. Add this to dry ingredients and mix well.

Cooked playdough

Materials:
500 mL (2 cups) flour
150 mL (⅔ cup) salt
50 mL (¼ cup) cream of tartar
50 mL (¼ cup) oil
400 mL (1⅔ cups) water
food colouring

Instructions: In a bowl, combine the dry ingredients. In a separate bowl, combine the oil, water and food colouring (use lots of food colouring to produce an intense colour in the dough). Combine the wet and dry ingredients in a saucepan and cook over medium heat, stirring constantly, until the dough comes together into a ball (this should take about 5 minutes). Knead well to help cool the dough.

Also Available:

®MR. DRESSUP'S
Things to Make & Do

For parents, teachers, babysitters, and daycare workers — more than 50 creative play activities designed for children under the age of five.

Kids Will Learn How To . . .

- **Make their own finger paint, playdough, and a wonderful new texture paint called Drizzle Goo.**

- **Make a ziggy-legged spider puppet, or a letter carrier's bag and box.**

- **Create exploding colours with eye droppers, watch beans sprout, and make Happy Sandwiches.**

And Much More!

ERNIE COOMBS is well known across the country as Mr. Dressup, star of the CBC television program. **SHELLEY TANAKA** is an author and editor of children's books.

Published by:

Canadian Broadcasting Corporation
Société Radio-Canada